AF251429

by Joanne Kyger

JOANNE KYGER

JUST SPACE

POEMS 1979~1989

ILLUSTRATED BY
ARTHUR OKAMURA

BLACK SPARROW PRESS
SANTA ROSA ~ 1991

JUST SPACE: POEMS 1979–1989. Copyright © 1991 by Joanne Kyger.

ILLUSTRATIONS. Copyright © 1991 by Arthur Okamura.

ACKNOWLEDGMENTS

Grateful acknowledgment is made to the following publications in which some of these poems first appeared: *Bombay Gin, Coyote's Journal, Intent, Peninsula,* and *Temblor.*

Black Sparrow Press books are printed on acid-free paper.

LIBRARY OF CONGRESS CATALOGING-IN-PUBLICATION DATA

Kyger, Joanne.
  Just space : poems, 1979-1989 / Joanne Kyger ; illustrated by Arthur Okamura.
    p.   cm.
  ISBN 0-87685-835-3 : — ISBN 0-87685-834-5 (pbk.) : —ISBN 0-87685-836-1 (signed cloth) :
  I. Okamura, Arthur.   II. Title.
PS3561.Y35J87   1991
811'.54—dc20   91-23552
                                                         CIP

for Donald

Table of Contents

. . .Two Empty Container Stories

Just Space: Poems 1979–1989

■

You believe this stash of writing is "scholarly"?
Out of this we deduce . . .
From this we can see that . . .

I know it's a detective story of passions,
dinners, blood stuff around which the history of our lives
crank.
So enough of that tune I was singing there
further back, I'm up to date with the day-glo goods
of modern historical revelation, barely a day old.
It's the hungry growing of the future who wants to know
if *you* know. So what

about that deer in the backyard eating down the as yet
unborn apples. A little deer go away dance? bang
bang on the pots and pans? when just last summer it was
a heart-stopping glimpse of nature's larger grazer?

You *fence* it in.

■

A few days later at the washtub
        spritzy subject on the fine high jinks
Sum up time, exams
            Caw caw Caw Caw Caw!
            These three black crows have lots of news
         overburdening the other sounds
         newly arrived in this location
         such as myself five minutes ago
a definite need to be reassured
        that the present has always existed.

The Depressed Ennui before 11 A.M.

Now's the time to catch it in words, those pungent
rebuttals of "Hello, I'm just sharing my heart for breakfast now."
And it is time the Goddess of Compassion had her incense lit.

And from her inner lit path, she made her way looking
for her shoe. The dog had taken it.

And now off the top, I present you with seaside memories,
and an adventure to boot.

                       The memory part is meandering
along the channel as the tide rushes in
    And the man with the secret life gets swept right along
under the pilings of the houses, and fights back to land on the
        rocks.
           He walks back to the lady on the towel,
           immersed as she is
           in the newest freebox soap opera, she has just become
               aware
           of the danger of the situation. He lays down
           and goes to sleep.

■

Stripes of red, black, and gold.
So essentially I'm at home today
        trying to get the garter snake
    out of the wash tub
        without picking him up.
                How much time
        can I spend
regaining these refreshing circumferences of the day.

The importance becomes so slight
    with desultory trip downtown and back
A half a peyote button, a little break
    for erotic fantasy; David Hockney, painter
    in New Yorker interview seems very productive
and social at the same time this takes me to my own
    book shelves for a two o'clock cruise of Brautigan
on the top shelf.

            And thence to elmer glue surface
of Robert Duncan being mounted by grand gold lion a la 1958.
And also artist of above, Madam Nemi Frost Hansen, reclining
        on honeymoon,
peeling slightly.

            The news comes in by telephone,
gee, am I far away? Contemplating Larry & Susan's
Fire, and the excitement of ending this day.

■

Not much time left,
                now for this day's
            entry into type
                    a half shot into Baba Berrigan.

I'll check my wiring, get my veins relaxed, recover from the
        reefer
                downtown with M. Rafferty
                            just happy I'm here.
            What do you think of me?
                    Abalone sheen
                            strikes lightly
            Whitey speaks so wisely on the inventiveness
of human life, excellent blue eyes.
The Dalai Lama in San Francisco yesterday.
                    I call Philip Whalen but he's gone
            down to Tassajara Zen Center
            but there's Buddhism in the Air anyway
            with its hesitant Orientalism
            in cultivation. Positive forward proof
        or relocation breath like me interested
    in prolonging history.

My how the days fly by in Life Time

So now the sun shines
                on Raggedy Ann. Light October days
                    of confrontation sagas
                                and specialties of the heart.

So now the little points of harrowed necessity.
The Poets of Bolinas?
                            Hurled against unresisting walls
into the neighbors' lives, therefore living
        in the same house, need these words to fly
past the sink, into the casual flower
        arrangement of the eternal surfaces
                for breathing in life, My life,
which still wonders at the relentless role
                of being born human, once again.

■

Surprisingly she fell back into a line that was surely typing.
It must be, she mused, as her eye followed regularly, left to
    right,
left to right again. It must be a typed manuscript, she again
    mused
from her early California background.

                        There's a new friend out there
and I hope he makes it. Newly transplanted and waving

in a friendly sinuous manner. It's getting freezing.

Haiku for Charles Berrard   on his 40th Birthday

Man get relaxed

Woman get permanent

Having a Grand Time with the Hot Shots
. . . or how I ran into my friends downtown.

    Well I'm back from New York poetry trip now and raring
       to go.
Read the new John D. MacDonald mystery. Duncan came over as
Donald was headed off to work late. Duncan had been drinking
vodka and peppermint schnapps the night before in the city.
We walked downtown and found a place to sit in The Shop
garden, safe from Aquarius John's loud entreaties to Larry
about something on the street. "I want to read your books."
Larry had been sleeping for two days at the Howard Johnson's
in Tam Junction to get away from him. He still thinks John
burned down his house. Shao joined us later. I was full of all
the names from New York, and quite happy to be back. I saw
Michael Wolfe tanned and without glasses in front of the
Bolinas Store and caught up some more names with him. Um.

The Life of Naropa   for Ted Berrigan

Born in 1016, Bengal.   Died 1100, Zangskar.

IN DREAM LAND WHERE I AM SITTING ON EVERGREEN ROAD, THE
    FLY
BUZZING AROUND THE ROOM, MARCH 26, 1980, AT 10 A.M.
    GAZING
THRU THE WINDOW AT THE BECOMING MORNING.

"A sentient being has taken temporary residence in your
    womb."
This is blissful, this is brilliant light, this is Naropa,
conceived at last by parents who await him with devotion
and reverence.

Thunder, earthquakes, and rays of light mark his birth. He
grows up super smart and sublime. Religious life or Lord
of Earth? Well, in secret he becomes a great scholar.
He sees the impermanence of life, this makes him sad, he is
eight, his heart is set on the Dharma.

            So he goes to Kashmir
to study, even though his mother weeps and will miss him. He
studies arts, medicine, grammar, epistemology and rhetoric,
and masters them. He returns home to Bengal with 13 scholars
of sutras and mantras. He follows the order of The Deeper
    Under-
standing of the Hidden Meaning, and The Doctrine of
    Nothingness,

and the various tantras. But his father thinks there is enough
study going on and it's time for him to get married. So the
scholars go home and he decides he can live a married life
in the Dharma.

But it will have to be a very special girl—unprejudiced,
clean, Hindu, practicing love and compassion, and is named
Vimaladipi. The ministers go out into Bengal and find her.
But her father says, We are Hindus and high caste Brahmins.
We don't marry Buddhists, even though I'm sure you are all
from very good families.

The ministers then lay down on his front steps and intend to
stay there until they die or get their request complied with.
The townspeople say, Let the girl marry! And Papa Brahmin
gives in.

With a gulp Naropa realizes the impossible
has been found and marries her when he is seventeen. She
listens to him with fervent conviction as he instructs her in
the Mahayana and she becomes his disciple.

After eight years
however, the samsara gets to be too much for him and they
        split.
She agrees all she does is beguile him and both parents allow
them to divorce. He goes to a hermitage and studies tantras
and texts for three years. He goes on to Puna in Kashmir,
is ordained a monk and studies more. Then he goes to
        Pullahari
and spreads the Buddhist doctrine for six years.

THE YEARS ARE IN TIME, LIFE TIME IS IN TIME. WE ARE TEMPORARY
BEINGS. THE YAWNING MOUTH OF DEATH GETS US ALL. WHAT
        SHALL
WE DO.

At Nalanda is the great university of Buddhism, with
its five hundred scholars. It is NAROPA they want as their new
head. He debates with the scholars, Buddhist and Hindu, and
      wins
over them all. "An unusual faith in the liberating power of
the Victorious One (the Buddha) has been created everywhere."
Seven hundred Hindus shave their heads and convert to
      Buddhism.
The banners are hoisted, drums beat, the great conch of the
Dharma is blown, happiness and joy.

                              He continues on there for
eight years. One day he is out studying and the shadow of the
ugliest most pathetic old woman in the world falls on his
books. Do you understand the words or the sense she asks
Naropa. The *words*, he replies. And she does a little happy
dance waving her crutch over her head. Hoping to make her
even happier he adds, And the *sense* too. Whereupon she falls
to the ground weeping, You are lying, you *don't* understand the
sense. Well who does, then, asks Naropa. My Brother, she
tells him, Go pay your respects. And then "she disappears
like a rainbow in the sky."

                    This he decides to do, even
though the congregation at Nalanda begs him to stay, for he is
such a graceful, accurate, powerful teacher of the Dharma for
them. But he knows he needs his own teacher now, and taking
      his
begging bowl and staff starts towards the east. But he can't
find his guru. Where. Where. He comes to a leper woman
without hands or feet blocking the path. He's in a hurry, he
holds his nose and jumps over her, at her behest. She turns
into a rainbow halo. Everything vanishes. Naropa doesn't
recognize his guru.

24

He jumps over a diseased mother dog,
who turns into a rainbow halo. "All living beings by nature
are one's parents. How will you find the Guru when you look
down on others." He refuses to help a scoundrel out, and he
too
disappears into the rainbow halo saying, "If you think you're
too
great to help me out, you holy egotist, how will you ever find
your teacher." He runs into a man tearing out the intestines
of a decayed corpse and cutting them up. "Have you seen the
Guru Tilopa?" "Yes, but first help me to cut up these
intestines . . ." Ug, Naropa doesn't, and from the center of the
rainbow light the man tells him, "You'll never find your Guru
unless you cut the ties of reference." Then the next horror,
a man who knows where Tilopa the Guru is, if only Naropa
will
help him wash the stomach of this live man whose stomach he
has just opened.

When he refuses, out comes the light, which
says cut the ties. And on it goes, with the daughter of a King,
refusal to shoot the deer, eat fish and frogs in the evening,
kill parents, kill his lousy habit-forming thoughts! A freak
show of human impossibilities tell him to free himself!

He starts to give up, thinking he'll kill himself, and be more
successful in his next lifetime. But Tilopa arrives to tell
him he's been there all along, in all those various visions,
all awful because they are Naropa's own hangups.

He tells him
now he is worthy to receive instruction, and now he must
uncover the Wish-Fulfilling Gem, the hidden home of the
Dakini.

What was that? Some fine lines for you . . .

Spiders, on light blue paisley
                    Daisies in blue art deco
Porcelino totem found in Florence market, with silver *ear*
      attached. *Lift*

the covering from the window, the mere room. Java fox trot,
time to *clear* the table . . . mucho mucho. Wash, bathe,

lay papers with meaning aside in new beds . . .

      Susanna presents Achille's golden dome mushrooms, a lady
in command of the wind.

                        Calming now about one o'clock
Marked, bespattered & understood

            and yet you're still not sure about me . . .
      all the time. Saying "There is something for you
      to learn." Being sentimentally engaged.

■

          Going out to water the garden,
row upon row rippled mountain ridges.
So then I cleaned the house for 4 hours
          damped it down and whisked most of it
out the front door. Glued
          Kwan Yin's head back on for the glory
of tidiness and freshly cut daisies

                    Conjunction action:
Hastily turn to Naropa, Hastily turn to Naropa.
          What is Naropa doing next
          in the scenario drama
                    of the secret bonsai society
          "Don't expect More."

It's June 22, evening summer solstice time, like to feel
engaged away from the pain of breathing right now,
          and wonder what your star fucking absence
is all about at this moment of bamboo buckeye hesitation.

Saying things like, If you could only
forget about yourself for a while and all the 'credit'
you think you deserve.
It's eight thirty in the morning.
Crystal drops crowding the tops
of the meadow's purple grasses
No Difference Here
from the freshest and best
and off to see Franco in the city
and maybe Philip too
and I wish all well
I do, I really do

■

          Definitely resistance
in understanding the complications of Naropa

Funeral tubs by the ocean with Mayan feet
Bodies laid face down, no lid
So children cannot see dead faces

          Left with insurmountable rising anxiety
     in desire for serenity
  that every day culminate towards some blessed
white light of continuity

          There, see now!
The wind is in the light of the sun

Back from Bisbee: or Clean Up Time in Bolinas

For one thing the sun has appeared as Bobbie Louise
stated it would, after five days of non-existence.
At about 10 in the morning, as I modestly predicted.
A few shreds of fog now at 11.

         The poets brought the rain
to Bisbee in the summer of drought, Friday night when
Michael McClure and I read.

         Returning to Bolinas, the house
seems overladen, and my duty to lighten it up. I go out
to the shed and find Dharma Badger's sleazy leather-worked
guitar case and feel like throwing it out, but don't know
where to throw it out to. So leave it beside the door.
This makes me furious enough with my thoughts of the down-
town burnouts. Even Bisbee with the last stronghold of the
poor white hippies doesn't have such a determined bunch
of sleazos. Persephone Jones needs something to do
except being the Queen of Green Death & Smack. I arrived
to open the Bookstore at seven a.m. She's seated on the
steps. "Did you bring the Beer?" she said.

The Proverbial Friday the 13th:
Bolinas Mysteries Unrevealed

Katherine Mansfield's life unfolds on the pages of
Antony Alpers' concern . . .

                  Judith Hawk relates her emotional
life with current husband to acquaintance of Bakery steps.
Waldo Works clothing flying off the hawthorn
on the yet to be cleaned up premises of the Community Center.
Dried out Christmas decorations still over the door, poison
hemlock in the planter boxes, and many other grungy items
too numerous.

            Koller's new wife Leslie and baby,
making chicken soup in the kitchen. Kearney and crew back
to Birch Road to build some more of his house. Dusty
windows. A violent apprehension

                  in the middle of the day. Sit down & talk
to some one.

        The path to maturity through the understanding
      of symbols . . .

                Instantaneously & Gradually . . .
Naropa asks his teacher Tilopa to instruct him . . . Naropa
    brings
some glowing embers and a piece of cotton cloth. Tilopa pegs
the cloth down & lights it. The ashes hold the form
of warp & woof. The form is there but it is cloth no longer.
The effective belief in the solid reality of an external object
is destroyed. There is no return into worldliness.

                  Tilopa shows
crystal clarity, the threaded net by which Mind is caught

in Samsara. The rare jewel, the rare jewel. Indivisible
from the top of the head. "To see the Ultimate in this life
is to have obtained the highest realization in Mahamudra."

■

You like it huh? You like that dulcet stuff?
                              Inside language school?
                    This is strictly last minute
she admired exultantly, and ran to the door, a mere twenty
        minutes
away from presentation of plum and eucalyptus, why not. All
        poised
beckoning in some "future." The electric clock
from the 30's childhood belongs to me. *I* am the I
of this writing which indeed I like to do.

                              Admiring Ted Pearson's
stepped back distance of focus makes inveigling pages. I myself
am taking off shortly. A courtesy visit in the sunlight. A
ridiculous past time probably. The slightest breath, the slightest
breath of air. See you.

■

Horrendous preferences

keep trying to figure out life

with the awareness of death: quel problème!

New Smell in the Writing Room

After nine years these walls are painted white; again
this heavily book bound room of mostly poetry
looks a little more lively and orderly in the yet
mostly unread pages of white.

All of a sudden they start to speak
out what's within them —sort of white noise
Africa.
This is when the breath of muse
breathes softly in my encompassing ears
So surprising in shiny new room
with somehow altered old friends
on still sagging shelves.

What Starts Out as a Halloween Buddhist Love Poem for John Daley

It takes so long to do things. For example,
two years ago I decided the pittosporum, a fast growing
light leafed bush reaching almost tree size, which has
grown very satisfactorily by my back door would do well
as a hedge to shade me from the almost certain future
growth of humanity to my right. This land is covered
by coyote bush and natural adaptation mesa growth.
I was of course completely reluctant to invest a nursery
plant to the heartiness of this wilderness, especially
if they cost $15 each. Wilderness being deer, gophers,
snails, mice, and lack of water.

But lo and behold, in the most
barren ground right near the backdoor's most vigorous
pittosporum, nature's own course of plants from seeds,
has transpired. It has only taken nine years for this
plant to get the idea it could extend itself elsewhere.
But I do think it got my message that its living form
was definitely accepted in my backyard, and I wanted
more of it!

■

Bob Creeley has died and he is to have a Tibetan Ceremony.
Only it doesn't appear that he has really died at all,
since he sits around commenting on the succeeding
          circumstances:

We are all in a wasteland, after destruction, like the end
of six hours of TV watching. We are in a farmhouse upback
in the sticks, somewhere. There are various plots and plans
of escape.
          But at the end, one face emerges clearly,
          that of a Tibetan man, about 50 or 60
          the etched lines of distinction in his features

     —I thought I could be his nurse
       & heart & soul
       and I see he is the leader.
                 He is much smaller than I
       I look at him emotionally,
       sexually . . .

■

       This year has been difficult to remember
which month I am in, in March I think October.
       I must be *gradually* coming
to enlightenment
    for the instantaneous has not happened to me.
The wind has barely started on this 8 o'clock morn
   and still drifts lazily in 10 o'clock heat.
    I've talked to Diana, Susanna S.
Jim Anderson, Ken Botto, Ebbe Borregaard, Bill Berkson
and Susanna A. So far
    this morning stretches thru hand from Journal
Oaxaca, and the increasingly difficult Life & Teachings
   of Naropa, and the right way to sweep a floor.
Now I go to transplant poppies
    like transplanting thought forms
     Step on a series of snails, pulp
  into ground,
      Where is their life
  Now, this instant after
    their previous form demises

■

              Holding on to the edge
      of the World Baby
Buddha's Birthday. Pour tea
       over assembled drawings of one finger
    UP, the other DOWN: Earth
and Heaven's 7 steps; wild radish flowers nothing
     too good for you, Kid.
  Kid.

On reading ENOUGH SAID, for Joanne (as Per Usual)

For Philip Whalen (as Per . . .)

      Calm Down!
              White crown sparrow pop-pop-pop-pop
                  By now
    it's *me*
they're interested in, 9 o'clock Thursday morning soft
warm sigh of light breeze rustles in interest.
       Naked Ladies
      are those lilies on leafless
    thick red stem, page two, to call
attention to the particular vernacular
seven years hence from whence you wrote that   and me
                  not yet having gotten
   not yet having gotten to page three

     Calm down again!
           I like to sit
with the birds in the morning back door sun and
if no other thoughts impede
          that's ok too, even what
        you're *supposed* to do
    in the grand tradition
     of empty content from mind.
        To 'scotch' it; ruminations
and ramblings from 'the mind' our big
      multi-media connection of aimless luxury . . .

It is in a wide green valley
We find a red tiled hut
Generous fearlessness & Skillfull compassion
with The Flame Tree

■

In my dream last night Deer Lady
                is dressed in human clothes
Someone wants to make love to her.
She resists
She is lying on her back
He persists
Her four hoofed legs are dangerous
He enters her
She kisses him
                Her lower jaw
          a deer jaw
Is pronounced

Thursday hot sun dries grasses to gold
                    Looking for the drapery
                to be lifted in preparation
            for the animal bridge, the 'wild' world
of land outside the door

Inflection

Rita was mad at me. At Lynn's opening she was wearing
her accordion pleated skirt, one of my favorites. I said
Oh you're wearing that skirt again!
                    Again was the hit word, Gwenn told me.

■

Yesterday when Diana drops me off on Evergreen
and I walk to the cypress hedge entrance
the mother doe and her two fawns are grazing.
                                    Alert
head up, one baby watches as I stop. Wild animals
give off strong ripply vibration auras, like eucalyptus
ready to catch the wind. They groom
each other, color of the dune grasses they stand in.
I am non-movement watcher. Bambi fawn
after eyeing me starts walking in my direction. Wow.
Sharp hooves. He's got his eye on Ita Siamese,
other friendly living creature, sitting
next to me.
            That's *who* he's interested in.

■

Fall has arrived with quick clear blue skies
and your Blue eyes left this morning
With lingering remarks and no cigarettes
                and the flowers glow with lush clarity
      after your birthday.

"Have you been drinking Brandy with Diana?" he says
upon returning home at the end of the day and finding
her in utter despair. Burt, the famous Siamese father
is gravely ill and getting worse. The adorable fawns
have broken thru the apple tree fence and have eaten
the lower branches, leaves and all of the apples. Blue
eyes himself has not had such a great day. Sport, the
trusty Toyota has broken down over the hill, necessitating
$100 worth of brake shoes, ring bearings, and flat tire.
The dentist wants $250 to fix a tooth. We're utterly broke.
This becomes a wail, a keen. Larry Kearney taps at the door.
                He reports the crazies
are going crazy downtown. Jane is talking to a tree, loudly,
and crossly. Melissa is screaming drunk. Penelope is reeling.
Presumably caused by one day of excellent hot weather.
                Looking at the stove Larry notices the Pea Soup.
Must be winter he murmurs. He's broke too, and invites her
to pick cucumbers at the Webers' on Friday, $3.50 an hour.
Life is tough. She chips a celadon bowl, and goes to sleep
outside, under Saturn's rings she cannot see, and two
falling stars in Milky Way's dense belt.

Towards morning she dreams she is given in return
for some service rendered a sword
                    with a Celtic cross on the handle.

Thursday
            Burt the famous Siamese father is better
and the spirits of the day look inviting. She assumed
the day before as fleeting phenomenology, and starts
the new day reving strongly.   Hip. Hip.

                    The Hip was strongly attended
by Gin John's Birthday Jewel in the Lotus.
                    It proceeded from summer's talk
under the garden umbrella to the lagoon channel
which she swam with vigor over
to the dreaded Seadrift Stinson sand spit.
And back, to The Shop, where the Jewel in the Lotus
was revived by Ed and a sunlit return of many visible
notables: viz. Bobbie Louise, Birthday John and Buddy.
The Jewel swam over her head, submerging her in what
became a simple gin drunk high.
                    At this point
she entered Smiley's and was saved by her constant
reiteration that she had "just swum the channel!"
Realizing her casual mind was bereft and on
an escape route she succumbed to going
to a birthday party with her new-found escort. A grand
mistake, now covered with green paint she bumped into.
At the party she sang loudly covered with green paint.
The others *really* knew how to.
                    I just live over 'there'
she announced loudly.
                    After a while she *was* there,
falling over the new garden bench.
Bon Appetit! her escort echoed as his Toyota bumped away
down the dusty night road.

■

Relax thy head
              oh Great King of the Forest

I am suffering from fantastic deviltry
That sounds like me
In the attic haunted memory of dream drama
Practically terrified
I go to get the velvet seat
And heater.

Window Ledge

Tiny light grey moth
    New Delhi bronze rabbit
        Roy de Forest dog
           Kwan Yin
  Lady of white,
pottery shards from Palomarin shell mound
Miwok obsidian scraper, gourd pebble
from Boulder Creek, silver and white
streaked rock from Santa Barbara
Light grey moth

Under the bark is Indian writing

On the Francisco Mesa
    Spanish Moss, rust pine,
  cigarette butts, brandy
Under the bark is Indian writing—

Good Manners

The Bodhisattva waits
until everyone is finished
before he excuses himself

■

     The Karmapa spoke to me from a center of light
"Your works will flourish"
Let us see his strength and pray
     for his well being.

World needs Lobelia to flash
together in the garden
     Golden Crown
will come to his call
     In the world beyond
Is this world

     Has come and gone
with pair of Osprey
soaring at RCA Beach
     while we light low in the foam
     while we lay low

■

Defying gravity
        the powerful serenity
                of Redtail waits
        to catch his snake mid wind
        rain storm late morning

Weekend

<pre>
                    11 o'clock on a fog
           laden morning
                   And I travel to Athens, Africa, & after
     I water the garden
                   the sun begins to break
     thru and the dazzling field of grasses wave—

I wave back. The sun fades . . .
                   so do I. Only to review
           18 hours later, Nearer
the solstice   Everyone running around
like crazy in the dark of the moon resting
           in grasses under the fog
                      and going from Yummy
           into the Sublime
watching for the red gold line of morning
                   to rise
</pre>

■

Morning is such a welcome time. It doesn't demand
much from the pocket— Some coffee, a cigarette,
and the day starts, full of optimism & clarity of hope
While the Muse holds her head, and the crazy Elementals
        hold down their wrath
lightly under the earth's surface.
                                    Some vague attention
            of wind stirs the golden oats
and Ita Siamese drags her breakfast rabbit over
        the roof three
times into the house and escorted out
            the door. While Aram Saroyan & W. S. Merwin
        debate the paucity of their fathers' feelings
in New York Times reviews,
                            the deer
        coming down the pathway still
    are my startled guests as this morning proceeds normally
    out of doors.

Back to School

                I'm off to work
                the day is clear
                Sexism & Zionism
                in the air
                            and I've got
                my gloves on
                                after days
                in which sweet satisfaction brewed
                        at Arthur & Simone's wedding, barbecues
                    and old petrified Whale bone
                  for Sierra Ring of Bone
                Zendo, new home
                for old Lew Welch memories
            to sit now, at ease.

Why can't we get our books together! Why is our Library
such a mess! Why is that lady so lazy!
                            Why do we get tired of caring
            about the Mistakes.

                    The heady anxiety of September's past—
                Lulled on windswept ocean bluff
                into deeper breathing—   seeing
            this same old self become mindful again
            and well.

Dream

I'm doing this poetry reading with Simone
and I have nothing ready to read but the funny papers.
So I make up a poem about the

       GOLD LIGHT BUDDHA
It has a sappy ending. There is no audience
response. The LIGHTS aren't even on.

Kwan Yin means a Person
who *sees* the *sounds* of the world
And perceives the cries of people
in distress.
               She can manifest herself
at will
       to help those mortals.

So Please Bring me the Light!

■

The heady day of sun wading in Bolinas Lagoon tops
the entrance into Fall
            drifts into sanderlings' one mind,
        banks skillfully and quickly
    in the air, and disappears, to reappear
and it's Terry Bell's birthday
            as rainbow comes thru shimmering air.

        As dawn approaches day I am reading
        HABITUAL OWN WAY
                    Three elderly painters in a large studio
                work at their easels simultaneously
        How can *I* earn money
                or make it travel
    to me again I wonder looking blankly off
into privet hedge whose discerning edges look
        blank blank blank back at me
                and I discover my own
particular habitual ennui.

November 19, 1982

Two crows in the pine are loud
                and talking when I walk out the door
on my birthday morning.
                            How generosity wants
to come from me today to friends with presence
as the sun dips in and out of showers
                        and I gather the year's first
                Amanita from the grove
down the street, sweet tasting beneath a bouquet
                of brand new Iris flowers

■

Dinner at Briarcomb, that Artists' posh retreat.
In an effort to make the hostess "relaxed" I refuse
utensils and the large damask napkin
and demonstrate how to eat
just with the hands. Quite simple.
                              Like they do in India!
Her name is Kate.
I sing K-K-K-Katy to her, to put her at ease.
          My absolute BEST worst.

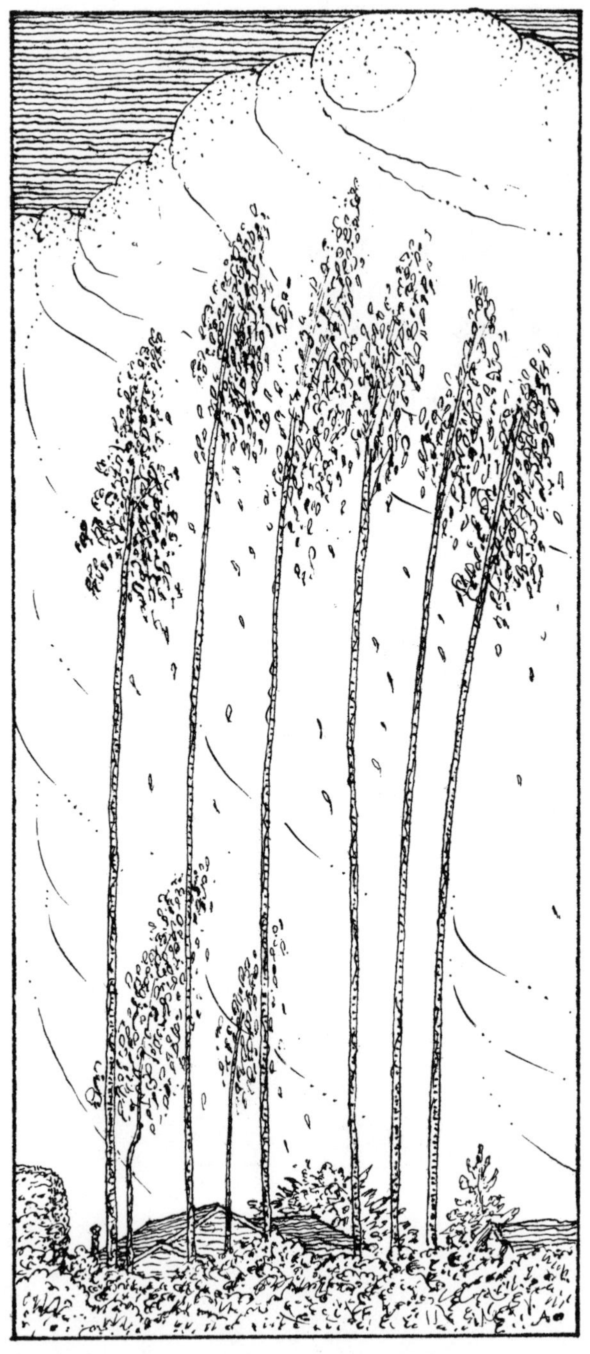

Thanksgiving

On Birch road is a large gathering including Anselm
from the city. We have found a companion for him
who speaks Finnish, since that is his native country.
We are very proud of our thoughtfulness.
She enters the party and we are all expectant.
She speaks to him in Finnish.
He frowns. He looks blank.
They turn away.
Both decide the other is from the C.I.A.

Dictionary's Guaranteed Success

There was no electricity. Simone couldn't type,
Shao couldn't listen to his tapes, many couldn't
cook, trees fell on houses, there was no time,
no radio, no coffee grinders.

It was Full Moon. Yes, you look gorgeous in
that purple slicker. There were candles,
there were wood fires, there was propane,
there was not food, there was the dictionary.

There was a *lot* of moon light.
There was Pleach, Nautch, Zamindar, Teniacide,
and Lumbricoid. And finally, there was Smiley's.

December 25

    Bill Brown has discussed his Christmas day
dinner for some time.
             We drink excellent wine
all afternoon.
             The little stuffed game hens
are in the oven.
             The afternoon passes
and evening begins. We check the hens.
The oven is not lighted.
We eat them anyhow.
The *wine* is still unblighted.

■

Glad to be back to you, now, soft fog
                              table perfume Narcissus
After November's full Scorpio weather rain makes us green
And out of $16 I lost 10 on the way to Smiley's
A shock that's now impelling me to bear the surfaces clean
            in this troublesome charming abode.

                              And there is still
ringing in my ears the woes of a future unperturbed
            without me in a flood of champagne tears
and misplaced mind
                  in the futility of chummy west coast enterprise . . .
But Voila! the $10 is found soon after
                              and enthusiasm goes
            its brittle way, in crisp windswept day, after day
with Poetry

Influences in Poetry

Dream:

      In a room getting ready for a party
with Dotty.
      Duncan MacNaughton comes in and says
"Stephen Rodefer is on his way here to kill you!
You'd better hide."

      We run to the bathroom
and lock the door.

      Come to think of it
Duncan looks pretty *strange* himself.

            "There's only room for one
            at the top of the steeple"
                     —Robert Frost

Back to the Life of Naropa

It's ghastly. It's been
going on for some time.
Sitting still for over a year, motionless
stiff as a log. No speech.
No thought. What's going on?
Naropa's teacher is not responding.

But finally he gets up and climbs to the top
of the fancy temple roof. Naropa follows him.
First words uttered: "JUMP!"
Naropa jumps to the ground.
And broken, lays there in terrible pain.
Great Disciple.
His teacher heals him instantly saying:
"You really deserved this, you clay pot!
Thinking there is an *I* inside that body
All birth and death and the stages in between
Must be resolved into the Radiant Light
of emptiness."
And goes back to his silent sitting.

Late Afternoon Rainbow

Coyote's Bow

Somebody is Getting Born!

Philip Whalen's Hat

I woke up about 2:30 this morning and thought about Philip's
hat.
       It is bright lemon yellow, with a little brim
    all the way around, and a lime green hat band, printed
    with tropical plants.
                 It sits on top
    of his shaved head. It upstages every *thing* & every *body*.
He bought it at Walgreen's himself.
I mean it fortunately wasn't a gift from an admirer.
Otherwise he is dressed in soft blues. And in his hands
a long wooden string of Buddhist Rosary beads, which he keeps
moving. I ask him which mantra he is doing—but he tells me
in *Zen*, you don't have to bother with any of that.
You can just *play* with the beads.

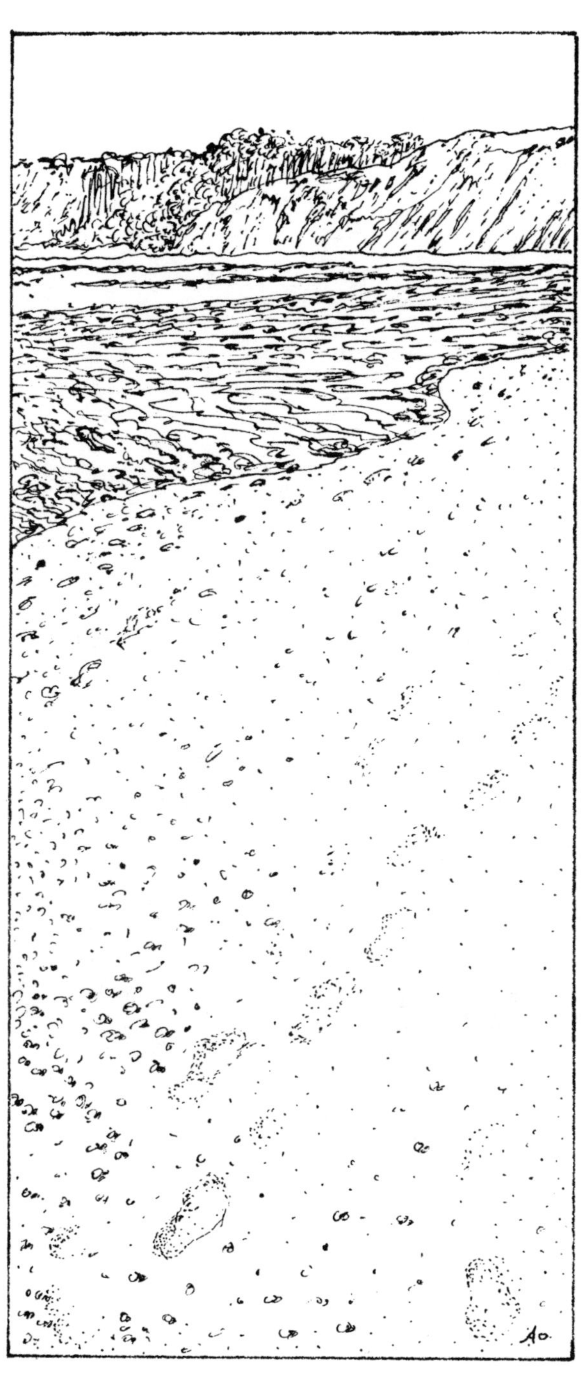

■

Robin Blaser's old plaster of Paris
Bust of Dante . . .
                    lent to me by
Paul Alexander . . .
now residing in our back guest shed . . .

Day after Ted Berrigan's Memorial Reading

Out back with Dante looking down his nose, kind of low
              limbed anxiety. Sigh. Don splitting cypress
          from huge pile felled last winter.
                              Is this the form

          I come home to? Yes, and beyond too, oceans
          of paragraphs reiterate the everyday story
          of amazing circumstances in life

                          And now the memory is mine
          of your welcoming encouragement,
                  greetings at the door, and that
          'Bolinas looks like Korea'
                          certainly an exotic touch
          of patience walking thru the streets. Enough!
                      I didn't travel
          to the city for words of you but kept it here pretty

well, your picture and some incense—   In due respect I was
          so sad now
                          Dante is in captivity
                  the night passed peacefully
              gliding up one current and down
thru another city.

■

"For the sake of the Kagyu teachings,
and the sake of all sentient beings,
breathe out a good rebirth,
                and breathe in any evil deeds
he may have committed

Help to guide him in his bardo state and wish
        he may let go
    of any samsaric desires"

                        —for Karma Kanchoe Yungdu
            the General Secretary of His Holiness,
                        the 16th Karmapa
                —from a service for his death
        on December 15, 1982 by Chogyam Trungpa

■

Fresh early morning light and again
I get a nervous phone call from my friend
           to see if "THEY" are in town this morning after
      the hair-raising paranoid last
   three days of getting busted for pot.
                              Cash crop blues
             No winter smoke blues.
                         Relief those plants
are pulled up, cast about, dispersed. The apples
      are falling
from the backyard tree. Spontaneous Persephone blues—
      bye-bye painting Mexican swimming pool blue
   in Shao's living room. Feed the sparrows some matzos
and watch the blue jays arrive, sassy
   friendly guys.

      I'm being chased by the pot police
   over a flat meadow dotted ankle high
with dandelions, clover and thousands
of very teeny pot plants.

Dream

There's a big Art Show in a large auditorium
consisting of pieces of paper with paintings
and sometimes printed circles & graphs underneath.
Louis Patler is standing in front of his piece—
A long list of words in the center of a large
8 foot section of paper. It has to do with
distribution of things by road and vehicle.
At the top of it shows where cast-off goods of metal—
like old trucks, and outmoded machinery—
all rusted and old, are dumped.
                A little further over
to the right on the paper, is where Louis Patler
got married to his wife. It's a silver dust store.
"We didn't even have a car, but she got married
in silver shoes—a silver suit and silver shoes"
he says.
              The rest of the words are technological
words down the page.
              "Oh *Louie*" I say.

Self Portrait

Ere I grow over prissy groves
And wander along with one last pine
So till me doomsday
    will I protest my jot
of discontent. And turning
    to that simple thought
of long ago sequestered cove
      find content on being beached
once more in heaven

January 12, 1984

             Hello '84
                        Ted won't
be in this year. Like dropping in.
                            I want
you and I to be
      special in memory's bright clear bobbing flows
    of paper and time.
                 I dream
of the worn
       obsidian arrowhead found high
    up in lagoon channel cliff side
   where the ground used to be.

■

The dream is dreaming
Something different
          In its delicious network
      the Center
              rests its longest pause
        in funny breath
                    breathe
                  UHHM OHHHHH
                  UHHM OHHHHH
                      Fog Horns
            On—   On—
                  Off   Off

May 2 Musings

I'm spaced after the liturgy of it all, the very
real issues a little larger than the personal
tete-a-tetes.
        Sort of rising anxiety working
with the pushy dimbulbs under 40 who want to
know it all while nothing, and I really mean nothing
happens I again explore the territory of nowhere
while the sun falls fondly
on the mesa ghetto . . .

Monday Afternoon May 14, 1984:

Now we've gotten that out of the way
We still have a ways to go
                            to take us thru the time
of this afternoon's wanderings
                      in the rooms of this house.
                            Two shades of red
matted behind Lynn O'Hare's new painting make it
too busy. The wind

is gusting horribly today. The Pacific Sun's
Lorna Cunkle refers to Bill Berkson's "ramblings
of an agitated mind" in his new book *Start Over*.

                            Gets me pretty anxious
too. Berserk looking dragon from Nepal gives me
a frenzied stare across the room, as afternoon light
falls thru it.
                No birds are out today. Definitely
change Lynn's matting, those reds are chatting up

a storm in the corner. A house is protection today,

against all velocity outside going 50 mph.

And this is a *famous* wind. It's already dangerous
            on 6 o'clock   TV tonight.

June 26

For Ted Berrigan

                    Unexpected gifts
             that liven the moments
          in our breathing days
               weighs
        heavily on me haunted "not free
        from the memory
      of others"
            Jogs the evening ceremony for you
    with lightning, thunder & rain, gusts of wind
brings your card and our collaboration
          almost a year old.

■

Giverny I am for Gee Verr Nee
                              I see
in purple and gold this time of year
              I am in long gold rays and I am in ah
I am in ah . . .
                    and I am in Long Gold Rays . . .
                                        So Great!
Do you think Tom Clark is really coming to town?
When he comes to town
                  You can say
                    I see you are coming in
      on the Long Gold Rays, the Long Gold Rays . . .

So profound . . .
              I met this Canadian Indian
who said he could bring the wind or make
    the breath of the earth rise with attention Me
Too said I, multi crystal medium thru ruthless talk
    I try to talk Numero Uno

                              July '84

Toeing the Line

                    So Hot!
Okay everybody take off your Toes!

                  Will the feet go
            to de Beach?? ah yas, yum-yum
                              Anchovy Moon mon
now wot?
            Looks like suspicious parts of animalitos
         regurgitated as leftover ocean bird dinner
      to swim in.
                  Well we are having supper now
                  and the air has
      the full moon leftover air.

                        August '84

Itsy Bitsy Polka Dot Review

Well, I'll never *sell* myself
out of whatever I've *got* which is, these days, folks
which is these days, folks
is um
darn hard to come by

Fall Equinox

                                    A lone
hummingbird sits on the limb where there used to be
two
            and now the hose is running
water into the garden where once you used to water
      the garden too why only yesterday
I saw you outside in the back garden watering some
plants with a watering can.
                              As I now water
the Iris I mess around with my thoughts
                                    Missing you
in Fall's purple blossoms my sleeve sniff! is wet

■

    Self Loathing & Self Pity
    I finish Somerset Maugham's biography
on almost empty Wharf Road Beach.
    —terrified, lonely, crazy, no religion, dies
  at 92.
      "I think a Tragedy has occurred"
notes Charles Reeves as I give him a ride up Terrace
as we pass Sheriff's vehicles in front of Richard Brautigan's
in front of Richard Brautigan's house. Well he's gone

away, maybe
    a robbery . . .

               October 25

November 19:   50 Years

> This year's birthday
>   Ham
> Hawk came down
> on the wood pile. Party
> about 50 friends
> 8 cakes.

November 25

> Going to plant
> Daffodils
> on Bill McNeill's
> burial site
> on his Birthday rest
> in Gorgeous Peace

December 7

> Wonderful Full Moon
> in this December sky
>   The Buddha
> gets enlightened
> Tomorrow

At Pt. Reyes National Seashore
              facing an expanse
     of starlings on green hill
        facing anxiety
        in the Tule Elk Range
        overlooking Tomales Bay blue & wind
   whipping around
      our truck God
Here is my art
Form and we find the herd resting
     itself laying
in the sun with lead
             Stag of 6 points and harem
   of 30 wives and children

              Sea Lion
         overlook frolic in blue warm
      waters of low tide noon and watch
      spumes of whales & their bodies
   break water '85
   and still alive!

The Wedding

Young pine tips & forget-me-nots

cow parsnips Hercules plant

Lupine

Narrative as Attention on a Rainy Sunday's Phenomenology

                And sweet sly good nights
          make me think light of you in the morning
          as you kiss me goodbye on this cheek
                    offered you on the muddy damp rutted road
          And you don't even *pay* me anything!
                    for the attention of Giotto's Limbo
                So I gave the last of your bread

              to the birds with some trace of envy
            on the block and when I came back it was all gone
          ready for a new
          feeding with full moon coming up over the slopes
                    where the cars come from
                          and I snuggle in the breast

          of enlightened harmony a week later.

■

Only one jay left after noisy conference of two
weeks ago on the search in the bare
buckeye branches there's some bread
For him he's busy like lone hummingbird looking
for springtime garnering

■

From here to Berkeley
          when the wind is sweeping
    the pollen up and around
my mind tries
        to focus on the reality
      of this evening's words

Past the briars that scratch
              the wrist on the way
    to Kwan Yin's yarrow patch.

                              Monday March 25 '85

Gin John

Michelle tells me
on God's Little Acre You
passed away last night to Kiss Me
Lightly when you Take me
Mother and Jump!

Nothing ever stays
Still on Tobacco Road but the Iris
Are rewarding to Memorialize this Moment
Of the Tibetan Airways. Look forward
In the chatty stopgap time. Breathe in, Breathe out.
No Breath
Anymore but Ours who Grieve
Your passing away
from Us
Grace! Copal! Iris! Eleusis!

May 2, 1985

■

Tuesday May 7

> The wind thru a field of wild oats
> How long does a second last

Friday May 10

> Nothing. Elm has never looked
> emptier or longer, hiking downtown
> with 20 pounds of Hearsays

Monday May 13

> A long smooth body is yours
> as I lay dreaming
> He sleeps dreaming beside her dreams
> Brown Iris, brown iris
>   Purple
> Lupine on the hills, as green
> fades into early summer.

■

Get up the screen of drinking herons
and dipping lions tossed over
with silken shawls

for Jim Nisbet's Wedding

Love Boat

Lynn doesn't want to miss the full moon tonight
As she saw it last night
                    As she saw it last night   an hour
earlier.
            At 8:30 settled on the Wharf Road Beach
We wait
        in the early dusk
                        with a bottle of special
Tequila Lynn has provided for the ceremonious occasion.
"We" are Donaldo, Bill, Lynn, me, & Tom the Eskimo man.
                Earlier we had picked up Tom,
the Eskimo man
                and Donald was surprised to find
            that he wasn't an Eskimo
But an Englishman.
                On the Beach we finally get in the right
seated positions next to each other. Make up
        Haikus about full moon. Bet on
where it will come up: empty beer cans
                            against empty
            clam shells
And watch the boat anchored out in the bay
                It seems to be gayly decked with lights.
We fantasize to wile away the minutes to moonrise time,
            sipping the ceremonial tequila
that it is a gambling boat
                with men in white jackets
            and ladies in evening gowns. An elegant
evening of entertainment out *there*

                    while we sit straining for moon to rise
over Tamalpais.
          Bill is starting to get impatient
     I think he is going to hail a Taxi at any moment
      on the empty sand beach
                              I hear a strangled cry from Lynn
down the beach.
                    I think she is being sucked up in quick sand.
          It's *Moon.*
                         Rising up over San Francisco!
Further south than we had ever dreamed.
          And Moon is orange, then with a black band across
like a pool ball or Moon in *mourning* And Moon
has perfect face Like *Man* in moon
                              And then Moon's
water touched lights reach across the channel to us
and there is Moon Head and Moon Body and each of us
sits or stands at the *feet* of Moon.
                              This week
I find out the boat that kept us docked in our places
watching the minutes away to moonrise
                         was a German freighter
which having unloaded its cargo of coffee in Oakland
               was anchored out there a few days waiting
for orders to move
          —named TEQUILA MOONSHINE
     Light Touched Waters

                                        July 2, 1985

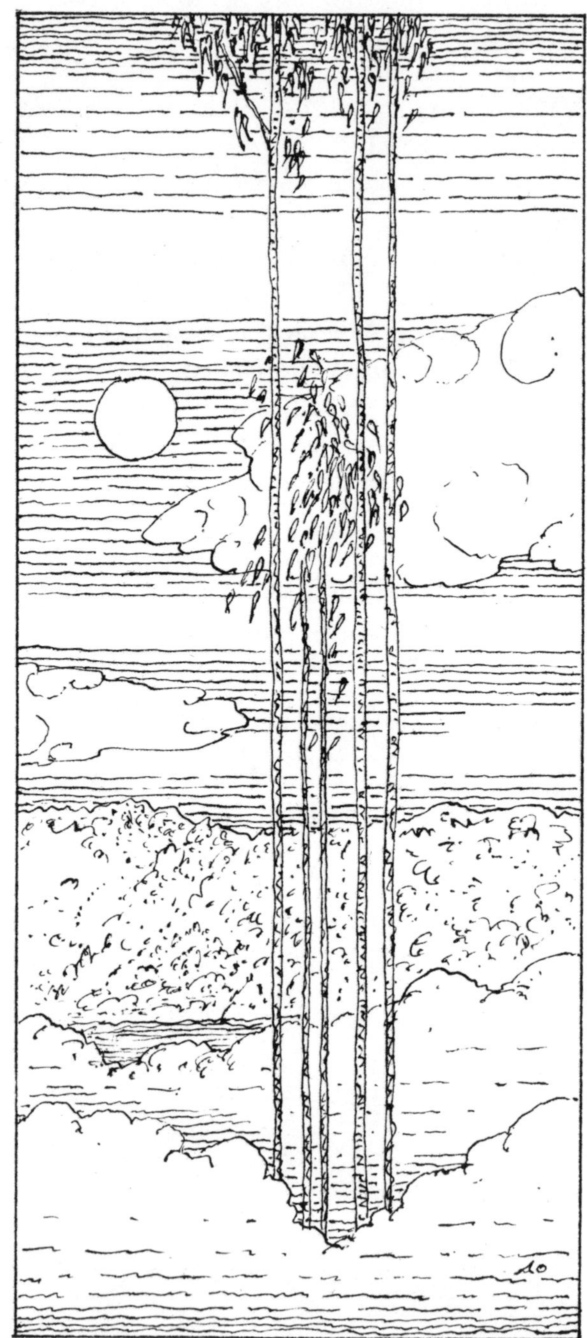

■

Ah it's socked in today boys heavy metal
and soft soft grasses

Yuppy Wittgensteins Arise!

And sleep again the puzzle
of dream
Gee glad you've got a horizon
to speak to You
are as humorous as the hospitality you enjoy
So you must go to the Dentist
just like all humans do
so similar to watching the moon
rise upon its occasions and all our normal
body functions.

August '85

Miwok Mandarin Bolinas Bamboo

What's that fur rug hanging over there—
Deer passing thru

Stealing the Religious Relic

Why was it so important to steal it away from the family,
tucked up inside the rucksack, run run, the legs are so
weary, the brother pursuing us with his gun, in anger
to get it back, you can't really steal the power, the
religious power of the relic that belongs to the family,
has a home. My comrade gets shot as he desperately tries
to board the small craft for his getaway. I am taken into
custody, stripped down.
           There are two relics. One is small
and wooden and sacred with ages. The other is a slender
metal three-pronged tripod affair which the German immigrants
fondle near the ravines of Acapulco.
           In the dark the
spotlight shows the passionate couple in a yabyum embrace.

August 21, 1986

■

You know when you write poetry you find
    the architecture   of your lineage   your teachers
  like Robert Duncan for me gave me some glue for the heart
Beats which gave confidence
                        and competition
       to the Images of Perfection

       . . . or as dinner approaches I become hasty
                do I mean PERFECTION?

                    September 17, 1986

The Enormous Sigh

The bardo of continuing limbo equals No Access

      to ANYTHING: Friends, land, time, inspiration

Total Misalliance as the biological clock ticks on.
And the Host of the imminent arrival
      says Come On Over, join the rest
of the Human Universe.

            What is going on
is very important at this moment:

Thich Nhat Hanh offers:

Breathing in, I calm body and mind
Breathing out, I smile
Dwelling in the present moment

And the clock ticks, only there is no time—
and longing for reconciliation
          is just that *longing*.

        September 1986

What is one to do . . . with what one . . . perceives . . . as actuality

                        I dunno
                             A mirror look today say
            compared with snapshot of beauty years ago, cobwebs,
            spiders in the corner reaches of childhood
            flashing green reminiscences
                                  Tending the corner of the past
                  which heart then warms to breath
            And correctly so for *care* which brings some peace
            today in muted light greens, warm browns and rose
                  of fall again.

                             September '86

■

"Oh Man is the highest type of animal existing
   or known to have existed
         but differs from other animals
     more in his extraordinary mental
   development than in anatomical
   structure . . ."
                  Well when I think of men
         I think of them in a sexual manner
Otherwise, I don't notice the difference, you know

being absorbed as *being* one just thinks 'people'
and not 'male' and 'female' so much as someone
to talk to. And how men are all

the same being born from Man and Woman and out
   of a woman's body commonly known as 'Mother.'

"And God said let us make MAN in our own image,
   after our likeness and let them have dominion."

      And "Nature may stand up
            and say to all the world,
               'This was a MAN!' "

      And then "I pronounce you MAN
   and wife."

         Daddy you is dandy

when you're here. Shrill and soft old Autumnal

      winds blow   and we are tucked below

the shallow soil where seeds spring
            up and wither quickly
      flirting madly.

        I've got him now,

the beautiful one for my part

of the year here in my dark
      and expensive underground
    all mine before he is shared

and killed again by the fearless boar
        he is hunting and torn apart
and his blood runs out and red roses and anemones

bloom   and it is spring and
      he is gone again

That man about town gone again . . .

. . . TWO EMPTY CONTAINER STORIES

■

Anything that is *created*
            must sooner or later die.
                  Enlightenment is PERMANENT
      because we have not *produced* it
    we have merely *discovered* it.
                              —Chogyam Trungpa
                                Died April 4, 1987

      Many years ago
I am going into San Francisco over Mt. Tamalpais
to read at a big Poetry Reading
given by Chogyam Trungpa in honor of the first visit
                  of the Karmapa.
I am very very nervous   I wonder if the car
            will make it
            I think I may die at any moment
When I get to the place of the reading
                              it is very gracious
            there is a bar set up back stage
The poets are given a little bottle
            with a hand lettered label
         saying "LONG LIFE PILLS
                  FROM HIS HOLINESS KARMAPA"
I am so nervous
I swallow them down right away and feel better *Whew*!
I ask Michael McClure, Aren't you going to take yours?
He says, I'm going to *save* mine.
Years later (still alive) I think of those pills—
They were little seeds

If I'd really done a wise thing
            I would have planted those seeds
                So there would be a whole bunch of seeds
            And everyone could have some
                    whenever they wanted them
So now what have I got?   the little bottle
                            of this story—
            and its own Empty Space.

■

DARRELL GRAY dies when I am in Mexico
I buy and light
            a votive candle in gold-trimmed glass
        for him, light it every night
and blow it out before retiring
                    I think of the candle as Darrell.
            During this month-long ceremony
          two tiny moths dive in
          and are enshrined in wax
      It is placed with the Navidad Creche
      and little by little
      the wax burns up.
                        I wash and polish the glass
and it shines
            I think Darrell is now an empty drinking glass
        and leave this devoted attention in Mexico
      for the next hand to fill up.

The Empty Shrine Buddha

If you grow your hair you save on heating bills . . .
Thus the globe rolls over

                        Poverty is something
Money can't buy.

                        Summer '87

Tuesday October 27, '87

Finest   first rain
Finest   first rain
            and the black lace mantilla
    the foamy ocean
   the exuberant show off
  General admiration and good will
 The man full of diamond light
           —as if many diamonds are shining inside him

        It's never really the same hunger
      is really over-fed accomplishment
     of the hungry ghost asking Is this really a life,
  a *way*, are you part of HISTORY?

A turquoise blue balloon   caught in the pine
       over the white
     shell beach of Tomales

Look deep and make a grateful show
       over that little silver beach.

Bob Grenier's Blackberry Pie

What else do you want
                besides us eating
            your blackberry pie

                            Gathering berries
So selfless   So virtuous
                    You tell me your aunt
            backed into a bear!

Looking over your shoulder
                I wish I knew what you wish to know
            about your economic records
            of the past five years
In   inspired continuity

A week and a half already from your famous
        blackberry pie

Remember the light purple blossoms opening up
        Opening up into star-crossed berries
        on a stiff vine
                        So far away only remnants
            of the pie down the road take me there

From the Jataka Tales

He   gave the king a charm
                        giving knowledge of all sounds
From that time he understood the voices   —even of ants
But if he gives the charm away   he dies
It is not good to destroy one's self
LIFE is the chief thing
What can man seek higher
And so he listens
To the voice of the ants: So little   is So Big

                              8 '88

Take it O Moon on the run

        Take it O Moon on the run . . .
O moon on the run
      in my back yard over the septic tank I don't
want to pay more taxes.
            I'm not on the money train
choo-choo advancing into financial
maturity ie Expansion. The same or *less*

that's fine. For me.

                8 '88

Narcissus

"Credit
I never get any *credit*
    for what I do—
No one *thanks* me
I do all these things
   for people
     and I never get any *credit*
I want to be *boss*
I want to be in *charge*
I need money *money*
I never get any credit
People don't thank me
I hate them. I hate this
  town
I am so lonely. I've never
  been so *lonely*."

AT JON'S HOUSE

January 3, 1989

Strike the impending muse   phew!

  'and not to search for the perfect poem'

amid the tumbled over cabin
—lessons of stability in utmost gale wind
      coming from unexpected direction
         of northeast fury

No, let us erase the worries the thoughtful worries
            as impediments of the Heart beats
where truly there is still wonder

with an offering of winter lavender's purple beads
      and graceful unfurled calla lily
            blossoms of the winter New Year

January 5, 1989

Ridge line silver mist . . .

                         hot sun on the elbow
       jazz on the radio
         Frida Kahlo self-portrait with parrots
        lays with possible distress on the floor
       until she is picked up and the intermittent rain
starts gusting

          Man leading his horse off
in the fields

          Social moves and nuances

I *knew* this was a day for rainbows
              in a field of raptors busy
        for lunch
         And so what's 'Buddhist'
       about all this

landscape consciousness
       and its fragile human frequency?

       'The mind is as blank
      as a bone on the beach
     when the tide runs out'

Company that's what
        it's all about entwined
      in the same air and waking
      in the same sun's dawn

January 6

Hot morning sun after frost . . .

> 'You just come here and take the cream
> off the top!'

January 16 Monday

What's that curling over there—
Incense snake smoke joss stick

You sit down and have an afternoon chat with a friend
You talk about other people, what they are doing
Maybe you characterize them, not exactly judge

them, but mull them over in terms of anecdotes
words, they're very ___________ .

Evaluating

January 24 Tuesday

Risky show-off shows internal bending. After the super-
bowl. What a way to go. In dream we are expanding
the house. This is a portable tool shed and will do good
for you to work in. Where are you now—hiding behind
the faces of others in dream you appear variously.
Woe is me if I do not recognize the subtle powers
of spiritual vibration pent up in the psychic center
of our being. Oh beloved, don't you want to know?
When the space is as empty mind, the flat meadow,
the ridge line. The ways things happen, and then
capitalize moments later. Entering into a dark tunnel
she was suddenly shocked. Nothing but darkness existed
around, pressing closely, firmly. Sit down. You
can see Nothing, the mind buzzing. Fruitful pursuit
of listening to breathing. Singular monstrosities
arise. Panic. Give me some relief, oh Sun, at least
I can see.

     It is significant
    to allow
associations, feelings, when they arise.

Longing for heart—must I sit awhile?
        All this time
All this time has gone by because time is old. Old
  -en days of lutes & fragrant gardens watching butterflies
     dance lightly, slowly the breeze
       ruffles the light silk garment
        of this lone sitter.

January 26 Thursday

Sheer impudence or just . . .
      'The ugly vulture eats the dead
          guiltless of murder's taint.
      The heron swallows living fish
          and looks like an ascetic saint.'
that which is well said . . .

You go to a place. . . and you go to a place of understanding. . .
      Do you have to move?

'Their presence was a guarantee of calm, an antibody
      to agitation.'

February 1 Wednesday

        Oh Rainbow
            charges the channeling
        of the heart is the pot
        of gold a flock
       of white gulls fly thru fades and disappears

I'm not really used to God anymore
Like is he any different
           from that Flicker out there
        flying & disappearing into the Broom

       Outward bound with fluffy
cold clouds from Alaska.
     A whole FLOCK of meadow larks
have arrived.

Saturday February 4

White sheen on open Bolinas ridge top
powdered white sugar
the whole long ridge
is covered with light dusting of snow
'this has never happened
                        before in *my* memory . . .'

Dazzling surf clouds snow
And the plum blossoms!

Donald took a picture of it
I tell Arthur Okamura via phone who says
HE has just loaded his camera too

I mean the ridge has been covered with snow before
But not this *much*. And certainly not in one's
own backyard on the mesa looks like frost

Looks like Alpine Pacific Village Picture Postcard
Actually it's very cold here and has been
        since December except in the sun.

And the whole shebang, the whole ridge line
        looks like your HAIR Duncan
Gleaming, silver, white. Happy Birthday.

                         —for Duncan McNaughton

February 6 Monday

It's soo cold the garden hose is full
    of ice this morning on the ex-president's
birthday.

He'd be gone for just a day and he'd
be on the phone to her about some little thing-thing—
they *were* very interconnected. I'm sure he misses
her more than she does him, now that she has
some freedom. Of course whether freedom from
daily routine is really freedom or not is some
thing else.

Of course routine is the earth spinning
                and the sun spinning every day too

Head spinning propped in hand spinning
        wondering   about Sufi Rumi's
    tall black hat that is a tomb.
'When between the lover and the Beloved
            there is only a poor shirt left
wouldn't you want the light to unite with the *Light?*'

So, now
        this brilliant cold, this freezing
        of water in teacups out of doors
Salute your departure? I guess
        you are still around in the only heat
for the day which is sun

February 7 Tuesday

The phoebe in the icy cold wind darts quickly
for food in the air while the flock
of meadowlarks pecking on the ground wander
near the house at the edge
of the meadow. Nothing stays still
for long they are gone.

February 15 Wednesday

> The phone is constantly busy
>   to you
>
> We're on the other side of time now
>   Heart
>   is such a memory
>
> it can't go away but gets fainter
>   Valentine
> of yesterday   Little peeper
> frog inside the house calls
>   to his friend outside where frost
> comes every night
>
>   Although a green
> lushness is returning water

February 16 Thursday

It's like regular now the weather
        I mean is warm
    symptomatically sitting on a stump
in the sun   a stick of red incense
        . . . no one's here right now but we'll get
back to you later . . .

February 16

Post Valentine

Dee Dee & Diana:
What was it I ate
I won't tell you
  I just want you to
Dwell on it.

February 17 Friday

                    Mist   on the orchids
         and Mist   across the ridge   warm
     sun at the door   come in

Death Valley Desert Notes

in memory of Harvey Brown

With depressing & unexpected news . . .
Into the new moon
Green rock strewn oak dotted hills
Into Joshua Tree desert
How quick
How grieving
Better by Shoshone
Picking up by Zabriskie Point
One being climbs up inside another
                    for the revolution in art.
                              Signals of old
news on the unexpected desert rock
     A huge explosion
of clarity makes a hole 800 feet deep

And now it's awesomely silent
And there is a Raven Witch
                    Where shall we camp

I mean we are walking on an old stone beach
          when we see the horned lizard
And there it is again! the old newspaper rock
And the heat, and the sand dunes
          and the youthful exuberance of the artist's
     pallet in green
          russet, yellow red oxides in the hills

So, remembering to chronicle
            events economically
      and learn how to sit

      properly were what I thought important
   to learn from this space and respect
      and awe majestic old time news

Printed July 1991 in Santa Barbara & Ann
Arbor for the Black Sparrow Press by Graham
Mackintosh & Edwards Brothers Inc. Text set in Goudy
Old Style by Words Worth. Design by Barbara Martin.
This edition is published in paper wrappers
and a hardcover trade edition;
125 numbered hardcover copies have been
signed by the poet; 26 signed lettered copies
have been handbound in boards by Earle
Gray; & there are 11 special hardcover
copies signed by the poet each with an
original drawing by Arthur Okamura.

Photo: Allen Ginsberg

JOANNE KYGER is a native Californian. She attended the University of California at Santa Barbara and in 1957 moved to North Beach in San Francisco. Since then she has published fourteen books of poetry and her poems have appeared in numerous anthologies and literary magazines. For the past twenty years she has lived in Bolinas, California. She has taught at the New College of California in San Francisco, and in the Poetics Program at Naropa Institute in Boulder, Colorado.

Well-known artist ARTHUR OKAMURA is a native Californian and old time friend and neighbor of Joanne Kyger. He practices painting, printmaking and sculpture. He is the illustrator of numerous books and teaches at the California College of Arts and Crafts in Oakland, California.